THIS BAPTISM JOURNAL BELONGS TO:

D.ane
_____

BAPTISM DATE

_____

some ideas of what to write about in your baptism journal:

- -HOW my interview went with bishop
- -HOW I felt right before I was baptized
- -HOW I felt during the baptism
- -WHO baptized me?
- -was the water cold or warm?
- -WHO came to my baptism
- -what do I remember from the talks
- -HOW I felt when I received the holy ghost
- -the first time I repented after being baptized
- -HOW do I plan to stay clean and pure
- -draw a picture of you being baptized
- -HOW are you going to remember the covenants you made?

—

Made in the USA
Middletown, DE
08 October 2018